THIRD EDITION

Spiritual Exercises
for the 21st Century

A WORKBOOK

Gillian T.W. Ahlgren

VITALITY

buzz, bliss + books

Spiritual Exercises for the 21st Century: A Workbook
Copyright © 2025 by Gillian T. W. Ahlgren
Published by VITALITY buzz, bliss + books LLC
vitalitybuzz.org

VITALITY buzz, bliss + books LLC publishes original creations to grow the mission of VITALITY Cincinnati Inc, a 501(c)3 education-based nonprofit: sharing holistic self-care from neighborhood to neighborhood, person to person, and breath by breath since 2010.

The opinions and ideas expressed herein are those of the author and do not necessarily represent the opinions of the VATRONS of VITALITY buzz, bliss + books LLC or the Board of Trustees of VITALITY Cincinnati. Any errors, of course, are solely the author's.

Every effort has been made to give credit to other people's original ideas through the text. If you feel something should be credited to someone and is not, please get in touch through our website and every effort will be made to correct this text for future printings. Thank you!

Julie Lucas of withinwonder.com created the cover and interior artwork. Thank you to Nancy Bradley, Barbara Donne, and Chuck Kohl for proofreading with such care!

We invite you to honor your mind, your body, your whole self. Do only what you know to be right for you. While the invitations offered here in this book, on our websites and social media, and in our classes are geared to be gentle and easily modified by the participant to fit the participants' needs, please consult your medical doctor or health professional before undertaking any practices.

ISBN: 978-1-954688-32-2

For Arthur Dewey and Brian Shircliff,
in loving memory of Magda and Daniele,
and for Michael, of course

in gratitude

to the VATRONS
who breathed life into this book
by sponsoring its publication

Elizabeth Ahlgren, Alice & James Ahlgren,
William Amrhein, Nancy Bradley,
Barbara Donne, Ernie Drott,
Frederick Hatchet, Ann Horgan, Kathy & Chuck Kohl,
Julie & Christopher Komnick, Lea Minniti,
Julie Murray, Marilyn Schleyer, Brian Shircliff,
James Siegel, Mary Zeller

CONTENTS

A Felt Knowledge of God
39

About This Book

Ignatian spirituality conveys energy, empowering people to see possibility and to change. Some of us know this because we have experienced or seen Jesuit high schools and universities where people learn solidarity and care for the whole person. Or because we have been part of Ignatian-informed pastoral projects where relationship with God fuels transformative action in the human community—organizations like the Ignatian Spirituality Project (which offers retreats and spiritual accompaniment to those at the margins in recovery from addiction) or service networks like the Jesuit Volunteer Corps for young adults or the Ignatian Volunteer Corps for individuals in retirement. Ignatius Loyola had a fundamental optimism about the possibility of human advancement, in large part because he had great confidence in God's commitment to humanity and the reality of God's love that is always stirring up goodness. "Go forth and set the world on fire," he charged his earliest companions, sending them into territories where their only way of communicating was by embodying that love in action. Our world today deeply needs the contagious energy of goodness and the creative, relational possibilities that Ignatian spirituality fuels.

As a deeply practical person, caught up in a passionate relationship with God, Ignatius was not concerned about articulating theological insights as such; rather he hoped to share a method or "way of proceeding" that could be developed, adapted, and applied as appropriate in different contexts. (In fact, in his correspondence with other Jesuits, when Ignatius would give advice in response to their questions, he often tempered his counsel with the proviso, "or do whatever seems best to you," an expression that signaled his desire that people always be open to how the Spirit might improve our human perceptions, instincts and responses.) What he left behind, the text that we call the Spiritual Exercises, is effectively a series of shorthand notes, written more for people who guide others through the Exercises than for people who actually experience them. The Exercises contain a profound invitation to enter into transforming relationship with the divine in the unique ways that that relationship unfolds in our individual lives. Further, the Spiritual Exercises provide an abundance of insights and exercises to help us live in community and in the world more sensitively, more justly, more equitably, and more sustainably.

In point of fact, Ignatius Loyola's Spiritual Exercises have supported the spiritual formation of generations of vowed religious and laypeople worldwide. It is no wonder that the Society of Jesus determined that supporting people's growing knowledge of and collaboration with God through the Spiritual Exercises was one of its four "universal apostolic preferences" articulated in February 2019. The principles and practices of the Spiritual Exercises continue to energize and sustain the work of Jesuit high schools and universities, retreat houses, and social apostolates, and they support the training of spiritual directors and pastoral leaders of the future. They empower us in critical social and spiritual practices like discernment, reflection, colloquy, imagination, and collaboration.

The Spiritual Exercises are rooted in spiritual principles and practices that transcend the Ignatian/Jesuit tradition, connecting the Exercises to broader schools of spirituality and to spiritual practitioners globally. Capturing these principles and helping people appropriate the habits that make spiritual growth an intuitive and "ordinary" part of everyday life is the goal of this workbook, now in its third edition. Like the Exercises, the workbook is divided into four sections, or four "weeks," that represent discreet stages in a process of spiritual transformation. While it can be used in conjunction with some experience of the Exercises—retreats of 8 days, 30 days, or other retreats "in daily life" with some form of spiritual direction relationship—the book is also designed to be portable, to accompany you in moments of reflection wherever you are, and to make use of the principles of the Exercises to jumpstart the changes in our lives that we and our world deeply need. Use the Exercises in this book in conjunction with your journal or a notebook where you can jot down ideas and return as new insights come to you.

Who was Ignatius Loyola?

Ignatius Loyola (1491-1556) was born into a Basque noble family, and he lost his mother at a very young age. As older siblings married and made their fortunes, he was sent to the household of Juan Velázquez de Cuéllar, treasurer to King Ferdinand of Spain, to be apprenticed as a courtier. When his patron died, he entered military service. Ignatius's strategy was to prove himself through service, in the hope of receiving knighthood and a position at the royal court as a reward for loyalty and bravery.

On May 20, 1521, at the age of 30, he was placed in charge of the defense of Pamplona against an attack by French forces. Severely outnumbered, Ignatius refused to surrender and played a leading role in rallying the troops until he was struck down by a cannonball that crippled him—crushing the bones in one leg and seriously wounding the other. After two weeks Ignatius's wounds not only were not healing, but surgeons brought in to monitor him determined that a second surgery, with a resetting of the bones, was the only way that Ignatius would live. He endured this second surgery but only grew worse. On June 29th he received the last rites and prepared for death, but then experienced a sudden turn and was thought to be out of danger of death. Anxious to begin his life again, Ignatius was distressed to learn that the way that the bones had fused back together left him unable to walk normally—much less advance in his career aspirations. After a third surgery to try to even the length of his legs and cut away parts of the bone that jutted out from the leg itself, Ignatius quietly realized that the bone-shattering blow to the leg had robbed him of his dreams of success and prestige in royal service. He would have to completely re-imagine himself and his life purpose.

Ignatius was then propelled through a long and slow recovery process. He spent about four months in his family's palace at Loyola, where he began to read a then-popular *Life of Christ* and a collection of stories about the lives of the saints. Despite initial lack of enthusiasm, Ignatius found himself engaged by these narratives, entering into their drama and gaining a new sense of possibility for himself. When he was able to get out of bed, he decided to engage a pilgrimage to Montserrat, where he experimented with a series of spiritual exercises under the guidance of the Benedictine community there. Wanting to immerse himself more fully in spiritual practices that could guide him to a different future, he settled into a cave at Manresa for a year of reflection, self-examination, and prayer that gradually crystallized his sense of vocation.

As a man of action accustomed to seizing opportunities and leveraging his autonomy, Ignatius had deep-seated habits that were hard to change, and it pained him to realize that his desire for success in the world has led him toward self-importance and arrogance rather than humility, generosity and compassion. He also came to understand that his personal desire for God was deeply entwined with the life and well-being of the human community. In addition to making changes in his own habits, he knew that he also needed to invest in the well-being of others. He began to cultivate habits of noticing and trusting the inner guidance of the Spirit that he slowly grew more able to access. Ignatius's time at Manresa gave him a spiritual strength and a fundamental optimism in the power of God that never left him. The building blocks of what became the Spiritual Exercises were born there, and Ignatius sensed a new calling.

Gillian T.W. Ahlgren

Emerging from this time, he sought theological education at the Universities of Alcalá, Salamanca and Paris, in his quest to share the empowering love of God with others. Ignatius's passion for God quickly drew others to walk together on a journey of growth. Eventually his earliest companions at the University of Paris banded together and formed the Society of Jesus in 1540. Dedicating themselves to the service of church and society, the Jesuits lost no time in extending their mission to educate and spread the love of God into the world, with the Spiritual Exercises at the heart and core of their way of proceeding.

Ignatius did not set out to design or write the Spiritual Exercises. They happened to him, causing a profound and empowering transformation in his life. The experiential knowledge of God he gained through prayer and reflection gave Ignatius a new sense of purpose, a vocation, and a set of spiritual practices that supported his continuing growth and his deepening partnership with God. We can easily liken his time in the cave at Manresa as an extended, life-changing encounter with the living God, not unlike the gospels' depictions of healing miracles experienced by the hemorrhaging woman in Mark 5, the paralytic lowered into the house where Jesus was visiting, or the man by the side of the pool at Bethsaida. Each of these encounters was not simply a healing event; it was also a personal invitation to make something more out of the rest of a life.

Collaborating with God and with Others:
An Introduction to Ignatian Spirituality

Ignatius Loyola was said to have an interior life characterized by a capacity to feel things deeply with a rich awareness of the presence and activity of God. He did not begin life with such spiritual sensitivity, and, as the previous biographical sketch suggested, we can easily identify decisive moments in his life, as well as the ways that spiritual discipline and practices bore ongoing fruit over time. Ignatius testifies to the dynamism of an authentic life lived with a keen desire to learn, to grow, to improve, and ultimately to serve a higher, God-given purpose. The Ignatian vision helps us to cultivate our capacity to notice and magnify the dynamic presence of God in ourselves, our interactions, and in the world around us. The empowering tools of the Ignatian tradition stem from a Spirit-informed self-knowledge that shows us who we are capable of becoming even as it is keenly aware of our foibles, struggles and the places where we routinely fall short of our potential. This kind of radical self-knowledge reveals to us and reinforces for us that we truly come into our own as we grow into a deepening collaborative alliance with the divine.

It is Ignatius's working premise that God has loved each of us into life and reveals to us, over the course of our lives, who we truly are. Ignatian spirituality gives us a way of knowing ourselves that encompasses both our potential as human beings and our partnership with God, inviting us more deeply into both and supporting our capacity to be instruments of grace, light, hope and truth in the challenging world in which we live.

To live in spiritual awareness is to live aware of and open to divine activity within us and around us. Such an awareness requires sensitivity, honesty, and a desire to live toward our deepest authenticity as human beings. As our energies and attention are directed ever-more away from the kind of self-awareness that stillness and reflection bring, we are more challenged than ever to cultivate this kind of awareness. The tensions and stresses of over-stimulation, sensory overload, multiple demands on our time and attention, and all of the other qualities of daily life in the 21st century are increasingly well-documented. Cognitive scientists are noticing and pointing out direct correlations between the over-stimulation and hyper-arousal induced by our technologically-driven environments and more serious psychological challenges: anxiety, depression, forms of addiction, exacerbations of clinical conditions, and physical health disorders. Numbed, stressed, and otherwise disempowered by the constant stimulation, our adaptations to our environments cause us to be more disconnected from the integration of our deepest human capacities: our ability to be reflective, wise, insightful, patient, kind, and compassionate.

Additionally, as we lose our sensitivity to the stirrings of the divine, within us and in the world around us, we become all the more vulnerable to lesser messages about what we need and want, about who we are, and about who we can become. Spiritual awareness then becomes a continual stimulus to truth and an empowering way of living in a world that seems to prefer that we turn away from our potential as human beings. Over two decades ago, Jesuit Dean Brackley cogently wrote:

> The gift of spiritual awareness that we can cultivate through daily spiritual practices is an essential, empowering asset to us today, as we confront ever-greater challenges as human persons, individually and communally. Interior knowledge is experiential knowledge, involving intellect, imagination, will, the "affections," even action... Most often it comes in

the form of a new insight and the development of a new feel for important truths about life. Interior knowledge means walking and dwelling in the truth. (Brackley, *The Call to Discernment in Troubled Times*, pp 23-4; cf. 2 John 4)

The practical emphasis of the Ignatian tradition—its invitation to us to "taste and see" the possibilities that a deeper alliance with the divine opens up for us—proves to be a profound remedy for much that is overwhelming in our world today. These spiritual practices do not give us answers so much as they support our journey forward on a path worth taking. They help us to engage a healthy process of deeper feeling and knowing: a "feeling-with" and a "knowing-with" that is the point of entry into genuine relationship with God and deeper human solidarity. To grow in "spiritual self-awareness" is to begin to glimpse, individually and collectively, our potential as human beings. It is to grasp the significance of events, to be able to see how best to commit ourselves to action, to know what is worth fighting for and what is not. Spiritual self-awareness is also relational. It allows us to know, in our bones, that we are not alone in what we hope and strive for, and that we need not reach toward our deepest aspirations alone. Both God and others are here with us, and there is a living, loving principle, a "Spirit" living within us, that moves and stirs and guides us, as long as we remain aware of and attentive to its promptings.

The Ordering Principle:
Our Orientation to God

*"The Exercises are, above all, a time for intimate contact
between God and a retreatant."*

Spiritual Exercises, paragraph 2

The spiritual principles and practices contained in Ignatius Loyola's Spiritual Exercises serve a single goal: our deepening collaborative partnership with God. It is from that partnership that we derive our strength, learn who we are, gain a new vision of ourselves and what we have to offer, and grow into our giftedness as human persons. It is a relationship that truly gives us life and breath and being. But in this day and age, it is rare enough to have a rich relationship with God, and we are often hesitant to speak frankly of our desire for God, our need for God, and all of the ways that our intimacy with God feeds and instructs our thinking, our actions, our decisions, our hopes, and our dreams. Ignatius's honesty about the centrality of relationship with God to our life can be, for us today, refreshing and even freeing. The centrality of God in our lives gives us a deep capacity to say no to what diminishes and dehumanizes us, individually and collectively. Moving us from cynicism, bitterness and fatalism, a daily, even momently orientation to the divine is both a strategy and a formula for vitality, meaning, and joy.

The practices contained in Ignatius's Spiritual Exercises reflect the primacy of looking honestly, thoroughly and completely at the "inner movements" of our hearts and wills—what we are drawn to and why, the patterns of our impulses, the consequences of our choices—all in order to move us toward greater "inner freedom." In light of the reality of human ignorance, fear, blindness, greed, malice, and violence, it is easy to see how powerful and important such honesty is. The exercises in this workbook can foster growth in honesty as you invest yourself more thoroughly in your relationship with God, self, and others, finding joy in companionship, solidarity, service, and communion. In short, the divine impulse, as it echoes its way in and through us, is a relational one, reflective of God's own relational way of being. Ignatian spirituality invites us to know a relational God who in turn teaches us loving and right relationship with ourselves and others.

In opening up for us greater contact, collaboration, and friendship with God, Ignatian spirituality offers practical tools for daily life and invites us into a relational way of living that draws us out of our smallness—our pettiness or narrow-mindedness, our selfishness, our smallness of vision or our cultural-centrism. By asking us to notice the dynamic movements of God in ourselves and in our world, Ignatian spirituality also helps us to know our place, both large and small, as we seek to live with greater intentionality into the wholeness of the human family. As you go through this workbook, I encourage you to see these Exercises as more than a set of individual practices or even a particular form of spirituality. They are an invitation to a deep and radical relationality. Not just a "solidarity" nor even a "friendship and familiarity" with God, but a form of relationship that reveals to us everything worth knowing about who we are and about who God is.

Relationship with God makes us and our world intelligible to ourselves, giving us a unique and very different framework for seeing things, understanding them, making sense of them, and,

Gillian T.W. Ahlgren

more importantly, responding and relating to them. We could say that the gift of the Ignatian tradition is that it not only reminds us of the presence of God in daily life, it also attunes us to the language of God, as that language takes form and shape incarnately in us.

Familiarity with God, encouraged through the practice of the Exercises, allows us to see, as David Fleming puts it, that "God speaks a language to us through our feelings." (David L. Fleming, S. J., *What is Ignatian Spirituality?* Chicago: Loyola Press, 2008, p. 89) This deceptively simple statement deserves consideration and exploration, because it is rich in practical insight but foreign and elusive to us as spiritual beginners. In practice, neither the "language of God" nor our own feelings are entirely intelligible to us. In fact, when we have (or think we have) little experience of God, that relational space can feel empty, frightening, even overwhelming. Ultimately it is relationship with the divine that makes us both authentic and intelligible to ourselves. The weeks of the Spiritual Exercises give us a structure and a disciplined practice to form the habit of relational contact with God. They are the tools to get us started.

But the tools do not actually do the work. What they really do is help us to notice a dynamic process already at work within the depths of our relationship with God. There comes a moment, when one is learning a foreign language, when one ceases to translate in one's head from one's language to the other; a threshold is crossed when the words begin to flow directly and freely without the "intermediate step" of needing to be formed first in one's own tongue and then in the next. Likewise, the tools of the Ignatian tradition move us toward the threshold of companionate relationship with God. As we set down the tools and simply present ourselves, honestly and nakedly, in the space of that relationship, we grow in authenticity and are gifted with a growing sense of God's companionate presence. Ultimately, it is that presence that begins to serve as our discerning guide as we sift, in prayer, through the layers of experience, feeling, perception, sensory awareness, reaction, intention, desire and all else that forms part of our daily lives so that we know what, in our experience, is deeply true and worthy of trust and what is not. What matters and what does not. What is worth committing ourselves to and what is not.

There is nothing more powerful than authentic relationship with God. Knowing ourselves as God knows us is humbling, empowering, vitalizing, transformative and absolutely revolutionary. Yet there is subtlety, delicacy, and profound tenderness at work in that graced, powerful space of connection with the Source of all life. Developing relational trust with God, self and others is a process that needs and deserves time, space, consideration, and devotion—it needs and deserves the best of us. For it is out of that intimacy that an authentic life springs forth and bears fruit.

A Place to Start:
The Principle and Foundation
and Some Considerations

We are created by love, in love, for love, that we might learn love from God and share love with one another.

The Spiritual Exercises are preceded by a series of notes, usually called "Annotations," that reflect Ignatius's observations and recommendations for people who oversee the Spiritual Exercises for others. They are, in effect, the notes of a retreat director, but they represent spiritual principles that Ignatius learned over time and wanted people to take into account before entering the terrain of relationship with God. The Annotations represent some of Ignatius Loyola's most fundamental assumptions about God, about human nature, and about reality. Arguably, paragraph 23, known as the Principle and Foundation, is the most critical of the Annotations. It establishes a starting point for engaging relationship with God. Consider this paraphrase of the Principle and Foundation (which you can compare with two other versions in David Fleming's *Draw Me into Your Friendship* referred to in the "Some Resources for Further Reading" section at the end of this workbook):

In God we find our origin, energy and goodness: a loving God who wants to share life with us forever. As we come to know who God is and what God wants, we can grow into more active collaboration with the One who wants the best, for us and for our world. The human community and the web of life, created in God's love, want this collaboration as well, and so we orient ourselves more completely to this desire: I want and I choose what better leads to God's deepening life, in me and in the world around me.

This premise—and it is a premise or point of departure that we are to test in the fire of our own experience over the course of these Exercises—encapsulates Ignatius's hope that greater reflection on our own potentiality and on the beauty and potential of the world around us might help us grow in our desire for the God who so desires us. Rightly oriented to "what better leads to God's deepening life in me" is to be open to daily life as a set of opportunities and gifts to be used wisely and generously, so that all around us can flourish in the way that God would want. It is also to recognize the reality that we do not walk through life alone, but actually, we walk with the One who loves us surrounded by others who are also struggling to understand how best to walk together.

The Principle and Foundation represents the first (and ultimate) consideration of the Spiritual Exercises, because grasping and internalizing it as a premise for life has implications for us, individually and communally, in both the proverbial "big picture" and in the daily details of ordinary life. Some have referred to the Principle and Foundation as a "compass" to help us navigate, and this is helpful, particularly when we acknowledge that we can continually and repeatedly re-orient ourselves and our lives so that they best serve our relationship with God and what God would desire, for us and for our world.

An adjective attributed to Jesuit Joseph Tetlow has proven beneficial in communicating the disposition that frees us to continually re-orient ourselves: "momently." The Principle and Foundation reflects a profound felt awareness and a commitment to recognizing that we are being created "momently" by our God in all concrete particulars. And if the language (either of "God" or of "creation") presents a stumbling block for our consideration, we can instead ponder the reality that each moment conveys both a set of circumstances to which we respond, some of which are chosen and others of which are imposed upon us, at the same time that these circumstances and the greater existential realities that transcend them present an arena of possibilities that we can develop, as individuals and as communities.

For the sake of our own well-being and that of others, each of us must consider what such a proposition—living "momently"— would mean. And much of the first segment of the Spiritual Exercises is oriented around such consideration. For me, living momently is a constant reminder to approach daily life with a disposition to live it moment by moment, deeply attuned to what is precious and sacred about that moment. Living momently allows us to vector ourselves continually to what is most meaningful to us—our deepest values, commitments and relationships—and to the ways that God is active in us and in our world. It also allows us to abandon trajectories in our lives that are clearly harmful to us or others, habits that serve no positive purpose, and any other behaviors that, subtly or not so, are not life-giving, to us and to to others. To live "momently" is to understand ourselves as being constantly created and re-created by God, but also by and in the concrete circumstances and choices of our lives. This understanding opens up powerful possibilities for positive change, even as it recognizes that, when we choose poorly or get sucked into dynamics that draw us away from our created potential, we do not always recognize the peril of our circumstances.

There is something very freeing and liberating about the realization that it is never too late for us to change! This is part of the power of learning to live in the awareness that God seeks to share life with us in each and every moment of our lives. Our lives are made of one such moment after another, each one of them capable of providing pivotal information about what God wants from us, with us, and for us. At the core of our being, we are part of a creative relationship that gives us possibilities that we alone could not even imagine for ourselves. We are here to dream God's dream (which is, concurrently, our deepest dream) into the world, in the concrete circumstances in which we live. Imagine what our communities and our world would look like if we lived toward the possibilities that take form and shape as we know ourselves in the light of our relationship with God. New possibilities emerge as a direct result of the choices we make each day. Each day we are asked to "choose toward what better leads to God's deepening life in me." (par. 23) This is the principle and foundation, and we are asked to make it the principle and foundation of our lives both for our own flourishing and for the health and well-being of the world around us.

The idea of "being created momently" asks us to attend with greater care to the momentary details of our lives, the intricacy with which our life is strung together, the causal effects of experiences in our lives, our understandings of the meanings of those experiences, the relational and social context of who we are and of who we are becoming in each moment of our lives. The Principle and Foundation is not simply about our relationship with God, as if that relationship were a private affair. We are meant to diffuse the love of God into the human community, especially in the places where people have been trampled down by neglect, abuse, injustice, and all that disappoints our God.

When we recognize that we are being created momently, this evokes a sense of awe and wonder at a God who cherishes and creates each one momently throughout each passage of our lives. Implicitly this idea suggests that our reverence for God and for creation, even for the mystery of ourselves and our relationships with others, grows and deepens with each step we take toward authentically engaging anything—seeing it for what it truly is. Scripture tells us to "taste and see" the goodness of God; this suggests that God's goodness is learned through experience and is constantly reinforced by experience after experience. In the Principle and Foundation Ignatius is inviting us to see and experience God in our lives; because God is a God of love, we will know that love experientially and want more of it. This "appetite" for God can then provide guidance for our every choice and desire, as the contemporary rendition of the last sentence of Spiritual Exercises paragraph 23 suggests: "Our only desire and our one choice should be this: I want and I choose what better leads to God's deepening life in me."

The Principle and Foundation helps us remember that the connection we have to God is the most trustworthy tool for navigating our lives and making daily decisions. Access to the grace we need for wisdom is both necessary and freeing. We are literally fed by the process of growing more aware of and more connected to God's presence in the world around us.

One final point: Obviously, to affirm that we "want and choose what better leads to God's deepening life in me" implies that we actually know what leads to God's deepening life, in us and in our world. We should readily recognize that knowing "what leads to God's deepening life" in us and in our world requires that we spend time getting to know God and allowing God to reveal Godself in our lives and in our world. As the Jesuit tradition recognizes, there are many, many ways to do this. But two important ways to start would be in quiet, tender, direct contact with God and also in encounter with those who show us God's face. The Principle and Foundation is, by definition, an invitation to constant growth, a warning against complacency, and a call toward improvement and advancement of the human condition.

QUESTIONS FOR REFLECTION:

What do you do to maintain access to God? How can you increase contact with the God who wants to teach you new things?

How do you understand yourself as being created momently? Can you identify some "moments" that have made you who you are?

What keeps you from choosing toward God's deepening life in you? How can you enlist greater support for God's ripening in you?

SPIRITUAL TOOLS FOR THE JOURNEY

There are three core spiritual practices that form the backbone of Ignatian spirituality: examen, colloquy, and discursive meditation. These practices function internally in a way similar to how, over time, the repetitions of physical exercises strengthen your muscles, balance, metabolism and acuity. As you become more comfortable with these spiritual practices, you can and should develop and refine them, so that they continue to empower your capacity to engage life with wisdom, compassion, and courage. Just like with physical repetitions, simply doing the same thing over and over will not lead to continual improvement. You will reach plateaus in which what has brought you to one level of fitness must now be enhanced or modified for further advancement. Likewise, these spiritual practices must be honed in order to continue to produce results, just the way that a physical exercise plan needs fine tuning and intensification in order to build muscle tone. The whole point of spirituality is to provide insight and foster growth; without courage, imagination and insight, repeated spiritual practices can sometimes lead to complacency or self-satisfaction rather than growth.

Teresa of Avila once famously wrote about the spiritual life: "Whoever does not grow, shrinks." Spiritual practices ground us and help us express our commitment and steadfastness, but they are also intended to help us see things that we cannot see on our own. We engage these tools not as a daily duty but as a way to be guided, informed, and inspired in the ways that we and our world need to change. They are both a bottom line (i.e., a daily requirement for maintenance) *and* a space for us to increase and deepen our contact with the divine, enabling us to know experientially the many ways that relationship with God sustains, enlightens, and empowers us.

TOOL ONE: The Examen
Seeking Guidance

The central daily practice of the Spiritual Exercises is called the "examen." The examen comes in an inexhaustible number of forms, but is practiced so frequently and routinely that in many circles it has probably lost its impact. For the examen to be effective, we should remember that the purpose of the examen is to give us a fresh perspective on ourselves and our circumstances.

It is common for people to be introduced to the examen as a daily practice, a remembering of the day and how it was experienced. In this practice, we review and explore introspectively the "inner workings" of the day, perhaps focusing on the particular moments that we sense have something more to teach us. Through the process of actively re-visiting the day's events we can re-envision them, seeing more of the context and reality of the experience than we could see in the moment. This process gives us the opportunity to notice dynamics, feelings, interactions, conversations, and other events in a more holistic way. It also allows such events and activities to communicate greater awarenesses or insights to us after the fact. For example, we might ask ourselves "How else might I have responded to that request?" or "What was it that I was feeling when I heard the news and how did that influence what I did next?" Certainly, it gives us the chance to explore "What might have been different if I had responded in another way?" and "Do I want to revisit a relationship or an issue with another approach?" Consistent practice of the examen leads to a greater appropriation of "inner freedom," the capacity to respond out of a space of greater inner awareness, clarity, and liberty to choose. There are many ways to do an examen and much literature on it. We prefer a non-formulaic approach with some questions for reflection and suggest that you try different examen formulas at varying times of day and add your own reflection questions as you think of helpful ones:

Some Questions for an Evening Examen and Colloquy

What did I learn today?

Where did my eyes linger? Where was I blind?

Where in my life do I need greater honesty?

What did I forget to say today? Who needed me to do or say something different?

What could I admit right now about my life that would prompt a hopeful change in me?

What differences did I notice in those closest to me?

Where am I neglecting myself?

What was God trying to tell me today?

Where could I have exposed myself to the risk of something different?

What did I avoid today? Why?

What am I doing that is not helpful to me?

What is crying out for my attention? How can I best attend to it?

Where do I need help—e.g., greater creativity, courage, support or imagination—so that I can engage change effectively?

When today did I feel most myself?

From the evidence—why was I given this day?

TOOL TWO: Colloquy
Seeking Conversation

Colloquy, as a prayer style, suggests forms of conversation with God and encapsulates more broadly the variety of ways we approach prayer with familiarity, humility, and openness to the possibility of dialogue. By "dialogue" I am not suggesting that we are supposed to hear particular words from God in the moment. Rather, I mean to suggest that we take a dialogical disposition in prayer, letting go of formulaic ways of praying and instead approach God more simply and naturally, presenting what is most deeply on our mind and in our heart. As we share more concretely our inner lives (e.g., hopes, dreams, concerns, fears, disappointments) with God, we may become more spiritually sensitive to the presence, response or movement of God in return.

Ignatius defines colloquy simply: "The colloquy is made, properly speaking, as one friend speaks to another, or as a servant to his master, now asking some grace, now communicating one's affairs and asking advice in them." (Spiritual Exercises, par. 54) This dialogical approach to prayer is a natural outgrowth of our openness to the possibility that we might discover, in God, our truest friend. It is precisely the experience of God as friend and compassionate companion that Ignatius had wanted to invite through the Exercises, and the prayer forms contained in them provide ways to engage that kind of relationship with God.

Gillian T.W. Ahlgren

Teresa of Avila, named the doctor of prayer in 1970, shows us what the practice of colloquy, deepened exponentially over the course of a lifetime of prayer, can become. For Teresa prayer is the way that we grow in familiarity with God, particularly as we gain experience, trust, and deep affection for God. Teresa teaches that "Prayer is nothing more than conversation with One whom we know loves us," and no real growth happens without it. In colloquy the various things that we might share conversationally with a friend or confide to their prayers (and even those things we might not dare say to anyone) are safely confided in a companionate, conversational way to God—who already knows what is in our hearts long before we do!

Both Teresa and Ignatius invite us to bring the whole of ourselves into prayer. As the fundamental backbone of our relationship with God, prayer cannot be a disembodied, disinterested conversation with an abstract entity "out there somewhere." The more of ourselves that we invest in prayer, the more we begin to have a sense and feel for the One with whom we are in relationship. Indeed, the more dialogical that prayer becomes, the more sensory and more incarnate it becomes. New forms of communication emerge as we give ourselves over more relationally to God. For some people, colloquy may already be a regular feature of their prayer practice. For others, it may be profoundly new, even quite disconcerting. For most of us, engaging prayer in this colloquial way will invite and challenge us to new levels of creativity and experience as we explore a more profound, holistic relationship with God.

What is the subject matter of our colloquies with God? Anything and everything that is worthy of your time with God. Ignatius offers a very simple rule of thumb that can become a helpful spiritual practice in ordering the subject and content of our prayer: as a prelude to the actual prayer time, we should always voice what we "truly want and desire" from God. As we sharpen our intention, focusing it more carefully on what most needs grace or illumination, counsel or aid, we learn a deeper form of spiritual and emotional honesty, with ourselves and with God.

As you begin the Exercises, try to engage a practice of colloquy daily, noticing, by the end of the Second Week, the impact of these conversations on your relationship with God. Start by writing up a list of topics for these conversations or reflections.

You might consider the following:

What would you want to know from God?

Where do you need counsel?

What has always puzzled you about your life?

What do you truly want or need to know or understand differently?

Take some time to consider some of the conversations you and God have never had. Are there any things that you have not really taken to God? Concerns, questions, struggles, fears, hopes, longings? Is there any issue of concern that you might be able to explore in a different way if you pose a new question to God?

Write up a list of topics, questions, or other conversations you and God have pending, and refer to it over the course of the week to help you begin to have some of these conversations. Continue adding to your "pending list" over the course of the weeks as more thoughts occur to you or new questions and issues emerge.

Gillian T.W. Ahlgren

TOOL THREE: Ignatian Meditation
Seeking Insight and Wisdom

Ignatian meditation is primarily discursive in nature—a form of prayer in which we engage or immerse ourselves in a consideration, a narrative, or an inner visual scene, with an openness to learning and being guided in our understanding and perception of reality. While not incompatible with other forms of meditation, the practice of Ignatian meditation does not involve abandoning thought, clearing the mind, using a mantra, or other techniques so much as directing the whole of our personhood to a subject of meditation or to being reverently in the presence of God.

Ignatius suggests that we always preface the act of meditation by asking for grace and articulating clearly and simply what we are seeking. The meditation itself begins with a kind of inner gathering of the senses and summoning our intellectual and affective capacities, so that they can be directed toward what we seek to know, feel, perceive, appreciate, or be with. In the sixteenth century this was called "recollection," a word that connotes a gathering of our inner resources and a capacitation of our being, so that we can be truly present to whatever is brought to our understanding. We also invoke our imaginative capacities, "to see with the sight of the imagination the corporeal place where the thing is found which I want to contemplate." (Spiritual Exercises, par. 47)

As we enter into the actual meditation we "compose the place"—that is, we allow layers of details to enter our awareness, so that we are immersed experientially in the scene. If the subject of the meditation is scriptural—say, the encounter between Jesus and the hemorrhaging woman in Mark 5, we would picture and invite imaginatively the crowds surrounding her, the dust on the ground, her physical appearance and physical condition, Jesus's response to her touch. And this would not simply be a visual imagining, but would involve the senses—hearing the words spoken over the babble and murmuring of the crowds, smelling and feeling the jostle. If the subject of the meditation is more personal, we would bring to mind details of a current circumstance of personal significance or concern, using the mind, heart and senses. In whatever case, the imagination creates the place or "picture," the memory supplies details and locates the scene in the larger human story, and the will engages our desire to be present to the significance of the moment.

As this recollection grows centered in the moment and the grace of God's presence is actually invoked, a colloquy or conversation can ensue. In his contemporary rendition of the Exercises, David Fleming writes that the colloquy, or our "intimate conversation" with God (or Jesus) can accompany our attempts to "put ourselves totally" into prayer. The intrinsic compatibility of the Ignatian spiritual tools is reinforced by the movement of the divine in creative, imaginative, worded and wordless ways. Fleming notes "I will find that I speak or listen as God's Spirit moves me." (par. 54) And again that "A colloquy does not take place at any particular time within the period of prayer; it happens as I am moved to respond within the setting of the exercise." (David Fleming, *Draw Me into Your Friendship: The Spiritual Exercises, a Literal Translation and a Contemporary Reading*, St Louis: Institute of Jesuit Sources, 1996, p. 49.)

Experimenting daily with these three core spiritual tools will bring greater depth and focus to your spiritual practice and contribute to a deepening relationship with the divine. They support your work through the various exercises proposed below.

Gillian T.W. Ahlgren

Getting the Support We Need:
Spiritual Companions

It is always important that we have people in our lives who are trustworthy companions and who can reliably help us to come to know ourselves better and engage a continual growth process that leads us to freedom and fulfillment of our deepest purpose. But particularly when we enter into new territories of growth and change, these companions are even more important. This exercise asks you to engage these relationships more thoughtfully and deliberately.

Describe what you believe are the qualities of a spiritual companion or ally of your deepest self.

Who would you identify as your closest companions or allies?

How can you increase contact with them as you engage the exercises in this workbook?

A Felt Knowledge of God

Ignatius's deepest hope for people engaging the Spiritual Exercises was for them to have a clearer sense of God's active presence in their lives, a "felt knowledge" of God's love. Re-familiarizing ourselves with our own stories can help us to remember God's presence in our lived experience.

Holding in our awareness with deep gratitude how God has "drawn us" is an excellent way to honor the journey of our lives that has already begun, as well as the relationship with God that is already in place and wants ripening and deepening. In this exercise, let's explore how we have become more aware and attuned to God's presence. Work with these prompts and then proceed onto the reflective questions:

How did God first make Godself known, accessible, or attractive to you?

Have you ever made a conscious choice to engage deeper relationship with God? What did that look like?

Jesuit David Fleming chose to title his contemporary reading of the Spiritual Exercises "Draw Me into Your Friendship," suggesting that the Exercises are a movement into deeper companionship with God. What do you make of that title?

Have you ever been "drawn" into God? Do you have a conscious friendship with God?

If you were to engage deeper relationship with God, what would need to happen? What would you hope for from that relationship?

Having engaged the above questions, now consider:

How do you feel as you consider your relationship with God? Can you think of a special way to express your gratitude for it in this moment?

How do you honor the story of your relationship with God? Do you celebrate or commemorate specific moments in your journey?

Gillian T.W. Ahlgren

THE EXERCISES:
A BASIC OUTLINE

The Spiritual Exercises are divided into four segments or "weeks," each of which represents a discreet set of considerations designed to generate questions, food for thought, and insights into life, human nature, and the reality of God. While separable from one another, the weeks have a clear sequence and an overarching flow that move us, holistically, toward generosity of spirit and a desire to contribute to the well-being of the human community and creation at large. A summary of the overarching movement and intention of each of the four weeks follows:

WEEK ONE

How do we know who we are, what matters to us, and why we are here on this earth? The First Week of the Spiritual Exercises provides us with an opportunity to ask the kinds of questions that offer deep insight into the meaning and purpose of our lives, shaking us from complacency, cynicism and malaise. While some call this First Week a time to reflect on sin and "fallenness," it is also a time to consider our lives as gifts and the extent to which, individually and collectively, we have been good stewards of the gifts we have been given. Such considerations are not abstract; they are done in order to awaken us to a deeper purpose and help us realize what we have to offer a needy world.

As we reflect on our own life histories and on the less savory characteristics of human beings (e.g., selfishness, greed, envy, arrogance, callousness, carelessness, recklessness, even violence and destruction), we understand and become sensitized to the "mess" we have made of our own lives and the "mess" that human beings have made of our world. Each of us is sure to see personal, social, and historical failings: the "smallness" and even error of our own self-knowledge, as individuals and as a human community; our willfulness and refusal, at times, to learn from our mistakes; and many other painful and troubling elements of the human condition.

In addition to the ways that we personally have fallen short, others have likely also fallen short in their appraisal and appreciation of us, perhaps failing to support us or our giftedness. We may also have to come to grips with experiences that have denied us of our human dignity—personally, socially or culturally. Perhaps we, too, have participated in the denial of the dignity of others. Week One awakens us to the reality of injustice and suffering in our world today.

As we become more honest about that and more aware about how much human suffering distresses and displeases God, we gain the hopeful and illuminating realization that perhaps it is not entirely too late. With the help of God, we can use what is left of our lives to be instruments of goodness in the world, remediating injustice and promoting the healing and flourishing of the human community and the planet. Using the language of "Higher Power" to refer to the divine and/or to the energy and strength necessary to overcome human weakness (as is often used in twelve-steps programs and recovery communities) can prove very helpful in this First Week. Such language intrinsically recognizes that we all need something more than the self in order to thrive.

WEEK TWO

If we are going to commit ourselves more seriously to the full realization of our human potential, individually and collectively, we will surely need a mentor and a method. Week Two is all about learning how best to be human: for example, what integrity and courage and compassion look like; how goodness in one person can ignite goodness in others; what the common good looks like and how to work for it collaboratively. From Ignatius's perspective, who better than Jesus could teach us those lessons? One needs only see the impact of Jesus's encounters with his contemporaries and consider deeply how different the world would be if we were to live in radical care of others.

The Second Week involves a deep exploration of the reality of the incarnation as a way of life rather than as a theological theory. We study the life of Jesus as students seeking to learn from a trusted teacher who invites us into deepening friendship and celebrates, with us, each step of growth towards freedom, dignity, and goodness. We also consider the alternative to that kind of growth—not just in the shrinking of our decency and humanity, but also in the falsities, insecurities, malice, contempt, and toxicities that swirl around our world. As we reflect on the healing and liberating impact of Jesus on others and become more aware of the ways that we ourselves have known and experienced God's goodness and encouragement, we realize how critical to our health and well-being that a genuine relationship with God really is. Our growing commitment to that friendship gives new life and new possibility. As we understand more clearly the consequences of our choices, we seek to align our vision, our goals, and our daily lives in purposeful and productive ways. We begin to consider who we want to become and how we want to live out our lives going forward.

WEEK THREE

Change brings resistance. As the work of the second week gives rise to deeper clarity about what it can sometimes cost us to do the right thing, we find ourselves needing more help, more solidarity, and friendships that are trustworthy. And as we open our eyes to the reality of unjust suffering in our world, we sense the call to shift and deepen our practice of accompaniment. In addition to "doing with" God and others, we learn to "be with," to choose into a love that leads to greater life. The love we find ourselves growing more capable of is a mature love personified in the courage of those able to stand up against injustice, to be faithful despite uncertainty and threat. We learn to become a bit more comfortable with silence, with uncertainty, with the risk-taking that love can sometimes require, even as we become more sensitive to the challenges of being a loving, visionary presence in our world.

If the Second Week teaches us what it means to be a disciple— that is, a student and friend of Jesus and an ambassador of the kind of human community that Jesus modeled—the Third Week teaches us the cost of discipleship, as our fidelity both to God and to God's vision for our world, finds us colliding with darker, more malicious forces in our world. As our eyes are opened to the work of making this world a better place, we seek to be among those who are willing to lend a hand, who will help others "rise up and walk," and who form communities of solidarity, compassion and care, in order to bring about greater courage, wisdom and goodness in the human community.

Gillian T.W. Ahlgren

WEEK FOUR

We see that the challenging growth that we have experienced over the course of our reflections is bearing fruit in an actual partnership with God—a Friend who never leaves us and whose support and companionate presence becomes even clearer to us as we experience and draw strength from the "closeness" of God in all of our circumstances. The spiritual practices that we have engaged consistently over the course of the weeks has given us deeper self-knowledge as well as deeper familiarity with the divine, and we feel a new confidence to imagine possibilities with "the One Whom we know loves us," as Teresa of Avila calls God. We allow ourselves to come to understand the divine as the Love that gives life and the love that is stronger than death, and this gives us a fundamental confidence and optimism about life itself.

In outlining the weeks of the Exercises, I have tried to provide a sense of their intrinsic movement and progression, even as I find that people with more experience with the Exercises begin to see them as somewhat cyclical and seasonal. We often have to re-learn lessons that once came to us with such clarity, while other insights take time to bear genuine fruit in our lives. I always say that one never "graduates" from the Spiritual Exercises! Once you understand the themes of each week, you will see those themes cycling through your life, your relationship with God, and your relationship with others, and you can use the framework of the Weeks to engage more deeply a time of challenge in your life. In effect, the Weeks themselves—their specific meditations, considerations, and insights—become part of your own set of spiritual tools for understanding, interpreting and engaging daily life.

WEEK 1:

A Long, Loving Look

In this first week of the Exercises we are encouraged to do a basic inventory of the trajectory of our lives, our challenges and our struggles, our gifts and our assets, our hopes and our dreams. We take this "long, loving look" at ourselves and our world in order to appreciate more fully the gift of life and become better stewards, individually and collectively, of what we've been given. We also take this look around us in order to find and take our place in a world that often tramples people down, a world that can both take our breath away with its beauty and break our hearts with its cruelty.

From Ignatius's standpoint, the best way to engage our world is to contemplate it thoughtfully, ask questions about why things are the way they are (and whether they do, indeed, need to be that way) and seek greater wisdom about how to make the world a better place. By honestly articulating our struggles and our need for support, Ignatius's hope is that we will reach out to others and will develop habits of deeper connection with the divine in our daily lives. Empowered by these relationships, we can then begin to change our habits and perspectives and grow toward our potential, individually and collectively.

Outline of Week 1

Ignatius's original language reflects sixteenth-century, pre-modern assumptions about God and the world, some of which we may find quite familiar and others of which may be jarring. The approaches and adaptations I am suggesting in the Exercises for this First Week translate Ignatius's intentions into our complex and challenging reality today. Their overarching goals are to encourage you to cultivate a desire for truth and goodness and gain clarity about what is working, in our lives and in our world, and what is not.

In the First Week of the Exercises, Ignatius recommends specific meditations, in an order of progression. (The paragraph numbers correlate to the place in the Spiritual Exercises where Ignatius recommends them.)

1. Reflection on the reality of sin and its effects (par. 45)
    a. Rejection of God's love: "whether we freely choose to respond to the love and life forever which God offers us" and a recollection of times that we have rejected God's love (par. 50)
    b. Inherited sin and the evasion of responsibility (par. 51)
    c. Reflection on "hell" and alienation from God (par. 52)
    d. Colloquy with God/Jesus (par. 53)

2. Further reflection on the impact of sin with a specific request for contrition (par. 55)
    a. Reflection on sources of life and sources of death (pars. 56, 59)
    b. The goodness and support of others (par. 60)
    c. Reflection on God's love as the source of my/our sustenance (par. 61): how can I respond to a God so good to me and surrounding me with the goodness of holy people and the gifts of creation?

Gillian T.W. Ahlgren

3. Further reflection on sin, with colloquy, and deepening desire for sorrow and grief for sin

4. Further reflection, with less active thought and more heartfelt silence

5. Reflection on hell and reflection on what is left of my life (pars. 66-71)

If I were to summarize for today what Ignatius wants you to observe and consider and gain a felt knowledge of, I would include the following sequence of exploratory questions:

Thinking about your life up to this point, where do you find yourself? What have you learned over the years about being human? How have you cultivated your gifts and talents? Where have you struggled? What regular contact do you have with God? If the goal of life is to live generously, stewarding and sharing the gift of life with others, how are you doing?

Taking a careful look at the world around you, how would you characterize "the way things are"—that is, how humans tend to behave; what motivates us; the extent to which people have access to both their basic needs and opportunities to advance and improve their lives?

How would you imagine that God, the source of Love and life, feels about "the way things are"?

Is what you notice and observe really "the way things are" or the way that humans have made them? What would need to change if we were to imagine a world in which life, love, dignity, solidarity, compassion and tenderness were cultivated and able to flourish?

What experiences have you had that have taught you about the power of love to change things? How might you access more regularly and more fruitfully the source of Love, the creative Spirit, the essence of vitality?

Who can teach you about your own capacity to love and to be a good person? How might you engage conversation with others in this process of becoming more genuinely yourself and embracing habits of goodness and growth?

GROWING IN SELF-KNOWLEDGE
AND SELF-AWARENESS:
A Basic Inventory

Before any significant change can occur, we need a clear, honest sense of where we are. Taking stock of our assets, skills, challenges, limitations, and opportunities is an important practice to engage periodically, in order to adapt healthily to our own needs and the changing world around us. Use several or all of the following prompts to take stock of who and where you are, writing as much as you want.

My life would be more satisfying to me if I…

If I had to name three areas in which I simply cannot compromise my beliefs or values, they would be…

Some of my deepest strengths are…

I struggle with…

I have been putting off…

I need help in…

An area of my life in which I find it hard to create a healthy boundary is…

Take some time to reflect on what emerged from the above prompts. What do you notice? Find a trusted companion to share about what you learned or engage some kind of dialogical prayer in order to gain strength to change.

A Slice of Life, Part I

Imagine that this circle represents your psyche. Fill it in with all the things that occupy your thoughts, your mind, and your heart: worries and preoccupations, undone tasks, concerns about yourself and others… anything that is taking up time or space inside you. Allow each thing that you draw in the circle to take up an amount of space in the circle that is proportionate to the space it occupies in your mind or heart. You are creating a snapshot of your internal reality in this moment.

Gillian T.W. Ahlgren

A Slice of Life, Part II

Now re-imagine this space, placing God at the center of it and only allowing "what better leads to God's deepening life in me" to take up space.

What does that look like?

*Take some time to contemplate both circles
and write about what you notice.*

Recognizing Habits and Patterns

We are often called "creatures of habit." Habits can be both healthy and unhealthy, and conscious and deliberate or so routine that we no longer notice them. This exercise asks you to consider some of the habits that likely need to be changed for your well-being and that of those around you. This exercise should be repeated periodically for review.

What habits routinely get you into trouble?

Describe each habit and some of the problems it has brought on.

How would it feel to be free of both the problems and the habit?

How can you enlist help in changing habits you have identified as ultimately unhelpful to your growth?

Mosaic: Piecing Together a New Story

In many ways, our lives are like a beautiful mosaic. Shards of meaning, which are at once signs of our brokenness and yet also represent significant moments in the overarching framework of our lives. In this exercise, the image of a mosaic gives us structure to explore and rearrange impactful moments in our lives, so that we can see our past a bit differently and allow the lessons we've learned through our past experiences to reposition ourselves and create moving and lasting beauty from brokenness. This Exercise consists of three steps:

1. Write a list of the significant moments in your life—the ones that are most meaningful to you, the ones that you most want to remember, and even some of the harder ones that have shaped you and helped you become who you are. You might begin by doing this review in a chronological way, thinking about the periods of your life, the people who have influenced you, the moments when something was realized, accomplished, or learned. These are the "shards" or "fragments" of the larger mosaic of our lives. But they are not just pieces; they are lessons and they are witnesses to a process of becoming. Contemplate them together and think about how they have gotten you to this point in your life.

2. Using pieces of paper, one for each moment, write about the moment and what you learned from it. You might use scraps from magazines or photographs to illustrate these moments. Once you have a collection of the individual moments, begin to move them around, positioning and repositioning them to consider their connections and the ways that, collectively, these moments have made you who you are and have brought you to this moment of your life.

3. Now consider the following: What insight and wisdom have you acquired, about yourself and about life, that will serve you going forward? What are you positioned to do now? What will you leave behind by way of a legacy that inspires others to make something meaningful of their own lives?

"That's Just the Way Things Are…": Confronting Fatalism

After over thirty years of teaching Ignatian spirituality, I have found that one of the most common resistances that students bring is largely unconscious: we simply do not realize how conditioned we have been by the world we have inherited. Even if we think of ourselves as broadminded, creative, and/ or optimistic, we still have difficulty fathoming the divine as a constant source of loving possibility. When encouraged to consider how God sees our world today or what God would want for us, students often look puzzled or sigh with a touch of impatience or condescension as they say, "That's just the way things are…".

South African theologian Albert Nolan, writing out of a space of entrenched apartheid, had something profound to teach, both about how entrenched our worldviews can be and about the kind of experiential confidence in goodness that Jesus can inspire. In *Jesus before Christianity*, he speaks about faith vs. fatalism, writing:

> Faith is… the conviction that something can and will happen because it is good and because it is true that goodness can and will triumph over all evil. The power of faith is the power of goodness and truth, which is the power of God. The opposite of faith is therefore fatalism. Fatalism is not a peculiar philosophy of life which once existed in some remote corner of the world. Fatalism is the prevailing attitude of most people, most of the time. It finds expression in statements like "Nothing can be done about it." "You can't change the world." "You must be practical and realistic." "There is no hope." There is nothing new under the sun." "You must accept reality."

Nolan goes on to conclude that

> Faith was an attitude that people caught from Jesus through their contact with him, almost as if it were a kind of infection… Jesus was the initiator of faith. But once it had been initiated it could spread from one person to another. The faith of one person could awaken faith in another. The disciples were sent out to awaken faith in others. (Albert Nolan, *Jesus before Christianity*, Orbis Press, 1995, pp. 39-40)

Thinking through how Nolan describes fatalism, when have you found yourself thinking "Nothing can be done about it," "You must accept reality," or "That's just the way things are…"? How prevalent are forms of fatalism in today's society? How do you find yourself falling into the habit of fatalism?

In what ways do you feel overwhelmed by the world you've inherited?

Over the next few weeks, try to notice the times that you fall into the habit of thinking that "there's nothing to be done" about something or "that's just the way things are" and ask yourself if that is the way things have to be. When you notice yourself thinking that way, ask yourself (and others) if there are different ways to approach whatever problem or situation has triggered a fatalistic response in you.

Finally, in what ways have you or can you "awaken faith" and open up possibilities for others, in order to contribute to positive changes in our world?

The Way Things Are: Three Examens

Create a quiet space and time to explore your current reality in three ways.

1. Thinking about your current personal circumstances, engage the following questions:

   What are some of the things that you most cherish about life?

   Do the people around you share and help you uphold those things that you value? Where do you see inconsistencies, conflicts, or obstacles to living with integrity and goodness?

   How can you inform yourself, through the experiences of others, about what is working and not working in the world around you?

   Where do you need a power beyond yourself to engage a helpful change in our world and make a difference in an area that needs changing?

   With whom can you work to make a difference?

2. Identifying a current situation or event that has distressed you, repeat this exercise by asking similar questions with respect to that situation:

   How does the concern I feel over _____ relate to what I cherish about life?

   How can I learn more about this situation, both through the experiences of others and through professionals who work in this area?

What could be done to change this situation for the better? (Be specific and comprehensive here in a reflection on possibility, without ruling things out a priori because of your concerns about cost or feasibility.)

What concrete steps can I take to make some kind of difference? With whom can I work to make a difference?

3. Thinking about the world around you, especially the earth, our common home, consider first these words from Pope Francis's *Laudato Si: On Care for Our Common Home*:

"Praise be to you, my Lord, through our Sister, Mother Earth, who sustains and governs us, and who produces various fruit with colored flowers and herbs". With these words, Saint Francis of Assisi reminds us that our common home is like a sister with whom we share our life and a beautiful mother who opens her arms to embrace us. This sister now cries out to us because of the harm we have inflicted on her by our irresponsible use and abuse of the goods with which God has endowed her… [T]he earth herself, burdened and laid waste, is among the most abandoned and maltreated of our poor; she "groans in travail" (Rom 8:22). We have forgotten that we ourselves are dust of the earth (cf. Gen 2:7); our very bodies are made up of her elements, we breathe her air and we receive life and refreshment from her waters.

I urgently appeal, then, for a new dialogue about how we are shaping the future of our planet. We need a conversation which includes everyone, since the environmental challenge we are undergoing, and its human roots, concern and affect us all. The worldwide ecological movement has already made considerable progress and led to the establishment of numerous organizations committed to raising awareness of these challenges. Regrettably, many efforts to seek concrete

Gillian T.W. Ahlgren

solutions to the environmental crisis have proved ineffective, not only because of powerful opposition but also because of a more general lack of interest. Obstructionist attitudes, even on the part of believers, can range from denial of the problem to indifference, nonchalant resignation or blind confidence in technical solutions. We require a new and universal solidarity. As the bishops of Southern Africa have stated: "Everyone's talents and involvement are needed to redress the damage caused by human abuse of God's creation."

All of us can cooperate as instruments of God for the care of creation, each according to his or her own culture, experience, involvements and talents.

How have you experienced the beauty of creation? Describe some moments in which you have been moved by the gift of nature.

Go for a slow walk in a natural setting and allow yourself to linger and notice the world around you. What do you do to maintain and enkindle your connection to creation?

How have you experienced concern, grief and/or frustration at the way humans treat the planet and its resources?

How can you engage greater care for creation?

Impacts

In the 21ˢᵗ century, we do not have to go far to imagine hell; we need only reflect deeply on some of the hellacious situations humans have created on earth. At this point, our own historical reality should give us a sobering caution about human nature and the human condition. Historians call the 20ᵗʰ century the Age of Genocide, a century characterized by deliberate, strategic and systemic attempts to rid the earth of certain racial and ethnic peoples. Even if we would like to think that human beings are basically good, it is important to recognize that humans have also consistently participated in the abasement and destruction of others. Taking time to acknowledge the darkness of human evil is an important dimension of this First Week, so that we are sensitized to the consequences of our actions, both for good and for damage and even death.

Using the framework described above for Ignatian meditation (composing the place and inserting yourself into a narrative or specific context), spend some time meditating on a space in which humans suffer because of the deliberate neglect and/ or cruelty of others. It could be one of many concentration camps during World War II (e.g., Auschwitz, Treblinka, or Mauthausen); it could be Cambodia under Pol Pot (1975-79), Rwanda in April 1994, or Bosnia in 1992-95. It could also be a space in which people are exploited by traffickers, subjected to torture, confined without having done anything wrong. If the spaces suggested above are unknown to you, use a survivor narrative, memoir, or legitimate historical source to inform yourself of some details. It is important to become aware of the very real shadow of human darkness that threatens to extinguish human goodness. Do not linger in this space of meditation for more than an hour, but use it as a way of understanding some of the forces at work in our world.

Gillian T.W. Ahlgren

As a counterbalance to the weight of the above meditation on human malice, choose a person you believe has had a positive and lasting impact on the world. Spend some time learning about that person: what challenges did they overcome and how did they grow into the person they became? How is the world a better place because of them?

Recognizing and Acknowledging the Pain of Turning Away

Our hearts seek meaning, resonance, and coherence. Infidelity hurts us far more than we often realize. There are many forms of infidelity that span a broad spectrum of behaviors and include what we have actually done that was unfaithful to our best self and to God (and perhaps to another or others) and also what we have failed to do.

In this exercise, you are asked to enter into a space of recollection and spend about 20 minutes thinking of a time in which you turned away from God and/or your most authentic self (often this "turning away" is a move away from both). Remember the situation in detail, recalling the circumstances and consequences, but, even more importantly, the feelings of that time and then what (if anything) you did to remediate the situation. Engage some form of colloquy around this exercise (before, during, and/or after), which might include journaling some of what surfaced for you. End with a consideration of what God, in God's infinite kindness, would want of you and for you. Then engage some kind of prayer for help in being more faithful to God and to the person God calls you to be.

Although this is a difficult exercise, it is an important one to engage a few times, especially in the First Week, but probably throughout the Four Weeks, because it reminds us of the constant need for God's mercy and grace for us to be the people of integrity that we aspire to be. It also reinforces for us the constant need for strength from God in order to be people of integrity and courage. As we realize both the pain and fruitlessness of "disengagement" from God—turning away in any shape or form from the strength and vitality that connection with God brings—we are far more likely to grow into a deeper and more permanent practice (habit) of turning toward (and remaining with) God.

Sources of Energy

Thinking about your daily life, what tends to motivate you? Where do you derive energy from? When you face something difficult, how do you find the courage to move forward? Is there anyone in your life who appreciates who you are and inspires you to develop your gifts and talents?

How do you resonate with the following poem sometimes attributed to Pedro Arrupe:

> *Nothing is more practical than finding God,*
> *That is, than falling in love in a quite absolute, final way.*
> *What you are in love with,*
>   *what seizes your imagination will affect everything.*
> *It will decide what will get you out of bed in the mornings,*
> *What you will do with your evenings,*
> *How you spend your weekends,*
> *What you read,*
> *Who you know,*
> *What breaks your heart,*
> *And what amazes you with joy and gratitude.*
> *Fall in love, stay in love, and it will decide everything.*

How has love been a source of energy in your life?

The Particular Examen:
A Method for Exploring Change

Consider several areas of your life (professional, personal, relational, spiritual) that need change. Return to the earlier exercise "Recognizing Habits and Patterns" for help in identifying some of the more critical areas in your life needing change so that the changes you identify will contribute in significant, meaningful ways to your growth and/or to your relationship with God. Examples of changes could be developing a habit or practice that helps you maintain access to your vitality and creativity or letting go of a practice or habit that you know is holding you back somehow from greater authenticity or from deeper intimacy with God. List some of the concrete, measurable steps you could take that would contribute to that change. You can use the chart below to keep yourself accountable to progress toward that change or adapt it according to your needs.

AREA OF CHANGE: _____

What are some of the reasons you want to make this change?

What benefits do you anticipate in making this change?

Concrete Steps	Days Engaged	Observations

Gillian T.W. Ahlgren

AREA OF CHANGE: _____

What are some of the reasons you want to make this change?

What benefits do you anticipate in making this change?

Concrete Steps	Days Engaged	Observations

Now try something a little more challenging: identify at least one habit that you have picked up that you know is keeping you from flourishing—physically, emotionally, intellectually or spiritually.

I NEED TO STOP: _____

What has this habit cost you?

What positive habit can/will replace the habit that you are letting go of?

Begin to set aside this habit in a way that is both effective and appropriate for you. Track your progress and observations:

Day	Observations
1	
2	
3	
4	
5	
6	
7	

Gillian T.W. Ahlgren

Reviewing the First Week

Where does the First Week leave us? It was Ignatius's hope that people going through the First Week of the Exercises would emerge:

Sensitized to sin (malice, discrimination, violence, indignities, callousness to poverty, needless suffering, and injustice)

Aware of our need for God—as a source of goodness, as a restorer of hope and strength, as a sustaining force for goodness and godliness in the human community

Grateful for a second chance

Ready to make changes in our lives (personally and communally)

Clear about the need for a good mentor/teacher/guide and companions for the journey forward

As a way of checking in with ourselves before turning to the Second Week of the Exercises, we should take a moment to do an examen in which we call to mind not just where we are but who we are in this moment of our lives. We can use a principle derived from former Superior General of the Society of Jesus Peter-Hans Kolvenbach. In a speech in which he reflected on "The Service of Faith and the Promotion of Justice in American Jesuit Higher Education," Kolvenbach said, "The real measure of our Jesuit universities lies in who our students become." This cogent sentence invites all of us to measure ourselves and our accomplishments in light of who we are becoming.

It could be that in the first week of the exercises in this workbook, you were given greater insight into who you have become. Perhaps some of those awarenesses were joyful ones and others were more painful. Before proceeding, I invite you to take some time to consider who you have become, who you are becoming, and what your most authentic self would be like. What do you want to leave behind? What is left for you to realize in yourself? Who will help you on your way?

WEEK 2:

Seeking Wisdom and Purpose

In the Second Week of the Exercises, understanding a little more now about what is at stake in our world, we commit ourselves to growing in wisdom and goodness. Embracing our freedom and capacity to choose, we set goals for our own growth, and seek examples of courage and goodness, past and present, for that growth. Guided by our relationship with the divine and with the spiritual companions in our lives who want our growth and happiness, this week brings inspiring lessons that give us a new vitality.

Outline of Week 2

Ignatius's intent for the second week is that we would consider the many ways that the life of Jesus provides us with a model for how to live. We consider especially Jesus's teachings, how he taught people to live and the kind of God that his life revealed.

Understanding Jesus to be the embodiment of humane qualities of kindness, care, goodness, and justice—the one who notices who is not present, who searches for the one who is missing, who attends to the one who is in pain, and who teaches and models responsible care for others and right relationships—we spend time reflecting carefully on Jesus's ways of interacting with others. We seek to learn from this example and to put it into practice—to cultivate our humane qualities and the gift of community.

The core meditations of the Second Week:

1. The Call
   a. Leadership (pars. 91-94): What does leadership really mean? Who are some of the most significant and inspiring human leaders? How did they stir people into action and promote human goodness?
   b. Jesus's invitation: (pars. 95-97) What is Jesus's invitation to humanity and what does that mean to you personally? How will you imbue the world with greater goodness and make this world a home for all?

2. Meditating on the Incarnation (pars. 101-109+)
   a. Does it make a difference to understand that God became human and was/is fully part of the human community?
   b. How did people experience Jesus?

c. What kind of community did Jesus create? Does Jesus invite us into a deeper, better way of being human?

d. What are the values of the reign of God that Jesus modeled?

e. "I have called you friends." What invitation does God extend to you today and how will that friendship bear fruit? (par. 135)

3. The Two Standards
   a. Strategies of the adversary (pars. 137-142)
      - habits, assumptions, priorities that functionally disable our ability to collaborate with God
      - isolation and enslavement
   b. Strategies of Jesus (pars. 143-147)
      - Uplifting people and reminding them of their intrinsic dignity
      - Modeling goodness, solidarity, collaboration
      - Sending people forth two by two to empower others

4. Three types of persons:
   a. A consideration of three approaches to life:
      - all talk and no action
      - doing everything but the one thing necessary
      - oriented to God's will in my life and in the world
   b. Who do I want to be and how do I want to be remembered? (pars. 149-155)

Purpose

List some people whom you admire or who have influenced you. What do you admire about them? What have you learned from them? What have they taught you about what matters most to you?

Do you feel you have discovered your purpose in life? How would you describe it? How has that purpose evolved over time?

Community, Solidarity and Collaboration: "We require a new and universal solidarity."

Returning to Pope Francis' *On Care for Our Common Home*, consider the following:

> "The urgent challenge to protect our common home includes a concern to bring the whole human family together to seek a sustainable and integral development, for we know that things can change. Humanity still has the ability to work together in building our common home." (par. 13)

> "All of us are linked by unseen bonds and together form a kind of universal family, a sublime communion which fills us with a sacred, affectionate and humble respect." (par. 89)

> "Many things have to change course, but it is we human beings above all who need to change. We lack an awareness of our common origin, of our mutual belonging, and of a future to be shared with everyone. This basic awareness would enable the development of new convictions, attitudes and forms of life. A great cultural, spiritual and educational challenge stands before us, and it will demand that we set out on the long path of renewal." (par. 202)

How do you sense and experience the invitation to make this world a better place?

Adversity:
A Consideration of the Forces that Disable Us

In the Second Week Ignatius asks us to consider the many ways that goodness—in us and in our world—has been disabled by forces of malice, deception, corruption and all that splinters or disintegrates our integrity and goodness.

In this exercise, we seek insight into the forces that disable us and all that we are up against by engaging reflectively the following prompts:

Describe some of the ways you have or have had false understandings of who you are. Were there messages from your family of origin, your communities (past and present), your culture, your significant other that diminished you or otherwise distorted your self-image?

Has there ever been a time that you have been seriously wronged? Perhaps by another person or by an institution or some form of cultural or systemic injustice? Consider whether or not this experience continues to have an impact on you and ask for the grace to be freed toward a deeper, more authentic you.

Have you ever compromised your own integrity? What process did you engage to regain it?

From what do you need to be freed in order to gain a new sense of your potential?

"I want and I choose what better leads to God's deepening life in me..."

Returning to the Principle and Foundation (par. 23) that serves as a compass to navigate our way through life, consider the ways that your access to God as the Source of Life and Love has been blocked, using the following prompts:

How have I been oriented to things other than God?

How have I been wrongly led?

Have I experienced deception, from individuals, from institutions, from authority figures?

Have I been influenced by cultural norms that have disabled my partnership with God?

How have I seen people (myself included) succumb to forces that go against my/our better instincts?

Based on the above reflections, what assumptions, priorities or habits can I identify that have disabled my partnership with God?

If the Adversary seeks "to isolate and enslave" us, how have I experienced or witnessed dynamics of isolation and being overcome? When have I been "stuck," overwhelmed or intimidated?

The Life-Changing Power of Jesus

Now consider several of the life-changing encounters that people had with Jesus as described in the gospels. Read deeply some of the following narratives, placing yourself in the stories, as a participant or observer, so that the power of the encounter can fill you.

Meditate with the healing stories in Mark 5. Recreate the story of Legion or of the hemorrhaging woman, putting yourself in their place. Consider specifically how contact with Jesus not only heals these individuals but restores them back into their communities. Reflect on the experience and journal a bit.

Meditate in a similar way with John 4:1–39, Jesus's conversation with the Samaritan woman at the well.

Based on these meditations, what do you begin to sense about Jesus? What is encounter and friendship with Jesus like, do you think? How do these people's experiences of Jesus resonate with your own experience of friendship/relationship with Jesus?

What new perspectives on Jesus have you gained? What questions would you want to ask Jesus? What help can Jesus give you now in a situation or situations that would benefit from conversation with Jesus?

The Power of Encounter

Take some time to consider some of the ways that you have experienced the power of goodness in your life. Consider and describe an experience in which a person has had a life-changing impact on you.

How did that person make a difference, and what qualities (e.g., fidelity, calm, generosity, wisdom, patience) did they display over the course of making this difference?

Allow yourself plenty of time to re-enter this experience, feeling its power and responding to the memory of this encounter with gratitude.

Metanoia: The Invitation to Change

The power of Jesus was not expressed solely in restorative encounters with others. It was also expressed in teachings about life and community whose truth empowered his contemporaries with a vision for how best to be human. Jesus's vision for humanity was of an inclusive community of care that affirmed the dignity of all its members and engendered generosity of spirit. In this way the common good could replace entitlement, privilege and egocentricity. This vision required personal and communal transformation but brought with it connection, lightness of heart, and purpose, as people began to experience what realizing their human potential felt like. Because Jesus's teachings challenged many social, cultural and even religious norms of his day, we often see him in conversation with authority figures, some of whom were threatened by the kinds of changes Jesus invited people toward.

In this Second Week Ignatius hopes that, through entering into the gospels, you will experience, in the same way that Jesus's contemporaries did, an invitation to companionship and collaboration that brings you a sense of belonging and greater fulfillment in life.

Consider one or more of the following passages in which Jesus offers commentary on human behavior. What kind of values and behaviors is Jesus advocating? What would the community around us be like if we embodied them?

Mark 10:13-31

Matthew 18:1-20

Luke 11:37-54

What Kind of Person Do You Want to Be?

This Exercise is based on a meditation that Ignatius introduces during the Second Week. Ignatius introduces a meditation on three sorts of persons. (See Spiritual Exercises, pars. 149-156) As he describes the first two types:

The first type of person struggles with inaction and comes off to others as all talk and no action. People in this category find it easy to talk about what they will do, but then do not follow through.

The second type of person struggles with avoidance. They often fill time and space with things that keep them from doing what would best support "God's deepening life in me" and the kind of collaboration with God that God wants from us.

> Reflect on some of the ways that you struggle with the above. Identify where, right now, you are failing to do something important and/or avoiding how God's life might deepen in you. Take some time to reflect with God about that, engaging a colloquy. Reflect on what you learn from this exercise.

The third type of person takes a different approach. This one says, "I may not know exactly what God is asking of me, but I do want to position myself to be available to whatever that is. I want to be sensitive and responsive to the movements of God's grace in my life."

> If what Ignatius is describing is not so much types of persons but habits that we can adopt, what habits could you embrace that would help you position yourself to be more sensitive to the movements of God's grace in your life and more available to what God might want to accomplish in and with you?

List the personal qualities that you most value and most want to embody. Consider the contexts, relationships and supports that help you to embody those values.

What conversations, with God, with yourself and with others can you have that will help you to manifest the self you want to be?

Make a list of conversational topics and create space for further dialogue with God, self and others over the next week.

WEEK 3:

Cultivating Fidelity, Commitment and Tenacity

The Third Week of the Exercises encourages us to explore the dynamics of fidelity and relationship when life puts us to the test. If the First Week has helped us to learn deeper honesty about what is truly real in our lives and the Second Week has challenged us to commit to what is truest and most meaningful in our lives, then the Third Week is going to teach us how everything in life boils down to our loving fidelity to the truth of our lives. At some core level, that truth emerges as the possibility of participating in an "unflinching love"—to be held in that love and to act in love, with love, for love, when the chips are down.

Outline of Week 3

The lives of many people, from Jesus to the prophets and martyrs of the 20th century, show us the stark choice that life sometimes poses: we can act out of fear or we can act out of love. In the Third Week we face that reality head on, as we are pared down and made vulnerable by life's demands on us.

In the gospels, Jesus models a vulnerability that reaches toward the other to create solidarity, hope and possibility when he makes his plea to his closest friends, while in the Garden of Gethsemane: "Stay with me." This becomes the theme of this week, as we consider the ways that we have had to face adversity, what we have learned, and the ways that we have touched the power and truth of love, keeping us alive in the darkness.

As we accompany Jesus in the final week of life, it is important to avail ourselves of insights from historical scholarship that Ignatius and other sixteenth-century figures simply did not have. Reading *The Last Week: What the Gospels Really Teach about Jesus's Final Days in Jerusalem* by Marcus J. Borg and John Dominic Crossan provides critical guidance as we navigate this difficult material.

The colloquies that we have been engaging as part of our prayer practice begin, in this week, to dissolve into deeper, wordless times with God, as our solidarity and friendship with God grows. We practice a "being with" that goes beyond words, like the ways that we might sit quietly with a loved one in a hospital room or try to express our solidarity and presence to someone in need. We come to God in our vulnerability and we experience the very vulnerability of God as we move toward that place of more tender intimacy with God.

As we encounter our own inner resistances to this kind of

vulnerability, we turn those, too, over to God, so that what we cannot do in ourselves might be done in us, through the grace of our relationship with the One who is love.

Being open with God about the moments of hurt, pain or sorrow in our lives (or in our current reality) is one way in which a greater solidarity with God might be forged. Ultimately, Ignatius wants us to experience God's solicitous care for us and the immense tenderness of that care, and there is no way to do that without allowing God into the most vulnerable and wounded parts of ourselves.

Something happens within us, however, when we reach into the deepest spaces of tenderness: we find genuine grounding in our connection with the divine. We learn that it does indeed matter where and with whom we stand. And as we stand in a space where our deepest truth meets God's deepest truth, something new is slowly forged. In a sense, the Third Week is a cocoon space, where a great transformation occurs. It is not just a personal transformation, though; it is the transformation that occurs when we commit ourselves to being with God and with all that God loves and wants to bring to fruition. In the Fourth Week we will learn even more about what that means for us. In the Third Week, the work is to be attentive, intentional and relational.

Because this week can become very particular and deeply personal for each person engaging the Exercises, it is important to set up and engage more support from others in this week, to go gently through the movements of this week, and to devote real time to gentleness with the material and any feelings it may stir.

The primary framework for moving through the Third Week is to grasp the reality of the suffering innocent one. Entering into that reality will challenge us: we will need to choose love over fear. We pray for the strength not to close our eyes or turn away, but to be people of unflinching love, able to advocate for those who suffer and to engage the work of transforming injustice, hatred, contempt and all that crucifies and destroys humanity.

The meditations for the Third Week include:

1. Reflection on the Last Supper (pars. 190-199)
   a. Noticing the way Jesus deliberately gathers people for a final meal and how much he shares of himself as he does (par. 191)
   b. Focusing on our empathy for Jesus and allowing ourselves to feel grief, pain, concern (par. 195)
   c. Reflecting on Jesus's vulnerability (par. 196)

2. Reflection on Jesus in the Garden of Gethsemane (pars. 200-203)

3. Reflection on the Trial and Crucifixion of Jesus (pars. 204-209)

4. Reflection on how to remain in solidarity with the suffering innocent ones (pars. 210-217)

Reflecting on Healing

Where do you sense the need for healing?

Intuitively, where do you know that you need to be met with tenderness? Can you confide and commend that place to God?

How can you share the balm of tenderness with another person in need?

Reflecting on Fidelity

Describe some of the ways that you have known God's fidelity to you. Write in detail about those times and spend some time after this consideration in a prayerful colloquy expressing your gratitude.

The Last Supper:
Reflecting on Community

The meditations that Ignatius recommends for the Third Week begin with Jesus's desire to gather his closest friends together for a shared meal and conversation. Read meditatively the accounts in Mark 14:17-26 and Luke 22:14-30, placing yourself in the scene as one who is part of this gathering. Notice Jesus's words in Luke 22:14: "I have eagerly desired to share this meal with you…"

In what ways have you known the consoling power of gathering people in times of turmoil or trial?

The Garden of Gethsemane:
Reflecting on Vulnerability, Friendship, and Betrayal

Review the beginning of Jesus's suffering, as depicted in Mark 14:26-72, reading slowly and placing yourself in the text. As you read:

Notice how Jesus asks his closest friends to 'stay awake with me.' What might this "stay awake with me" mean, then and now?

Notice the anguish and agony.

Notice the betrayal with a kiss of greeting.

Notice the dispersal of Jesus's friends as Jesus is taken away, and continue to notice the responses of Jesus's closest friends throughout the challenging days ahead: Who stays close? Who drifts away? How does where people stand impact what they see and experience?

What stands out for you in this reflection? How do you experience Jesus's vulnerability and steadfastness as things begin to fall apart? Place yourself in the position of various persons in the narrative. How have you acted toward others in ways similar to the ways that Jesus's companions respond to him?

After considering the above questions, you may also want to review the commentary on Mark 14:26-72 in Borg and Crossan, *The Last Week*, pp 120-135.

Gillian T.W. Ahlgren

A Meditation on the Passion

Review the details of Jesus's passion and death, as depicted in Mark 15, reading slowly and placing yourself in the text.

What stands out for you in this reflection?

How do you experience this narrative and connect to it in your own experience?

With whom do you most identify in the narrative and why?

After considering the above questions, you may also want to review the commentary in Borg and Crossan, *The Last Week*, pp 120-135.

"Who will hear my cry?"

Identify a person or group whose cries are not being attended to, consider what they are suffering, and compose a lament from their perspective. What would fidelity to them look like?

"Stay with me":
Learning from Others about Presence in Absence

Many of us already know something about what it feels like to lose someone we love. Grief, disorientation, paralysis, simply going blank: all of these responses (and others) are normal responses when we are confronted with loss. As we move through the Third Week, part of our work is to linger gently and respectfully in the space of loss, as a friend who remembers. In other words, as we continue to learn what true friendship is from our growing friendship with God, we are learning the strength or presence in a trustworthy relational context. This love that abides within us, whether or not a true friend is physically present, teaches us experientially that love is actually stronger than any division, even death. This is what Jesus's earliest friends had to learn after Jesus died. In the Christian tradition, the space we call Holy Saturday, marking the time between Good Friday and Easter Sunday, is a space between death and resurrection. We can consider this space as a space of more than a day, as a space in which live here on earth, with the many ways that we experience death and loss as well as renewal and abiding presence even in absence. Shelly Rambo explores this intermediate space of Holy Saturday as she develops a "theology of remaining." (See discussion in Shelly Rambo, *Spirit and Trauma: A Theology of Remaining*, Louisville, KY: Westminster/John Knox, 2010, esp. pp 102-5)

To remain is to maintain relationship in the midst of disruption, turmoil, loss, and even mortality. To remain with someone is to express in a profound way the radical power of presence—even when that presence is not physical, as Jesus spoke to his closest friends: "Remain in me, and I will remain in you... Remain in my love." (John 15:4, 9) To remain is to witness to and participate in the power of love.

Have you ever experienced a form of presence, internal or external, which communicated to you something about the abiding nature of love? Write about what you know, experientially, about that power.

Finding Strength

Dean Brackley, an American Jesuit who volunteered to replace one of the Jesuits assassinated at the UCA in 1989, once described how thinking about and feeling with the suffering of others allowed him to "feel less alone and more at peace…. driving home to me what is really important in life and where the center of gravity of the universe lies. It led me, slowly, to a new vision and sense of purpose. It taught me that I could trust that kind of consolation to lead into the light." If Dean Brackley is correct in saying that when we share the world's pain, the load begins to lighten for all of us, we have a way to become more a part of humanity's march, with its suffering, its hope and its joy.

Reflect on Dean Brackley's commentary on the Third Week:

> Suffering dehumanizes those who inflict it. But it need not dehumanize all who endure it or those who let it move them. Just as our joy is incomplete until we share it with others, suffering is more tolerable when we bear each other's burdens. Although that doesn't take away the pain, it helps. Above all, it generates hope and love in those who share others' suffering and in those who find their suffering is shared by others who care… The grace of the Third Week is to share God's grief over our wounded world… The focus is not on pain but on being with the one who suffers. (Dean Brackley, *The Call to Discernment in Troubled Times*, New York: Crossroad, 2004, pp. 175, 178)

Spend some time sharing your grief about something with God and seeking God's presence in your grief. Ask God for the strength and inspiration you need in order to move forward with greater serenity and joy.

WEEK 4:

Living with Grace and Generosity

The Fourth Week of the Exercises celebrates the reality that, in, around, and through the challenges of our lives, we are still here and we can still be loving people. In this week we consider and commit ourselves to living out all of the lessons we have been learning about the power of love and our own resilience as relational people. It is a "contemplation" and continual consideration of love in action in us. As we have experienced, having been faithful to the first three weeks, our lives are not over. We are continually graced with new possibilities, especially as we look beyond ourselves and ask for the grace to move beyond what limits us. This expansive space of possibility is created by our collaborative partnership with God, which we grow as we practice the habit of turning to God in everything, so that God's love can constantly bear fruit in our lives.

In this week, Ignatius urges us to contemplate God's love, not abstractly, but in ways that help us to see God's constant loving activity, God's generosity, God's desire to share life with us, God's desire to dwell and live within us and spill out from us in our own growing capacity to love generously. We look with gratitude upon all that has contributed to our being part of the adventure of life and with gratitude for all that we can be part of going forward.

Reflecting on Hope

Jesus's friends had to piece together the meaning of the loss of their teacher and find strength to embody all that they had learned from him when he was no longer physically there to encourage and inspire them. Review three stories in which solidarity and hope began to displace grief and fear in them. Begin with Mark 16:1-8, placing yourself in the narrative and feeling your way through it. Then read Luke 24:1-43 and John 20:11-18, placing yourself in the narrative as one of the characters.

Review some of the ways that God's presence has consoled you. Focus on a moment in which you felt that presence and spend time giving thanks for it.

Gratitude for Gifts and Graces

Consider and list the many things that you have to feel grateful for and joyful about. Be sure to dialogue with God after this reflection. Repeat this exercise daily through the week.

Reflecting on God's Love

In paragraphs 234-237 of the Spiritual Exercises, Ignatius Loyola asks us to reflect on various aspects of God's love. Spend some time considering each of the following:

God's love created me and makes me who I am. God wants to share more and more of the divine life with me, and God wants nothing from me except that I return love to God and to others. How does this knowledge feel and what does this knowledge move me to commit to?

God has not only graced me with gifts (e.g., health, intelligence, friends and family, personal qualities that I can share with others) but God also graces me with the gift of relationship with God to empower me in those gifts. How does this knowledge feel and what does this knowledge move me to commit to?

God loves me so much that God enters into all of the struggles of my life. There is no place in my life that God is not committed to enter into with me. "Like a potter with clay, like a mother in childbirth, or like a mighty force blowing life into dead bones, God labors to share divine life and love." (par. 236) How does this knowledge feel and how do I want to respond to God?

God's generosity overflows. The love of God is unceasing, and when we rest in it and receive it, we receive far more than we even ask for. Take some time to ask for the knowledge of God's generosity. Reflect on some of the ways you have experienced it.

In each of the above reflections, ask for the grace to be given deeper awareness of God's love and to be taught directly from God what God's love truly is.

Gillian T.W. Ahlgren

Reflecting on Collaboration with God

Review and consider a time when you were empowered to do something that you thought you could not do. How did that work? Go back into that time of your life in order to remember carefully and consider all of the details of the process of empowerment. Can you recognize the presence of God in that process? In what senses was God collaborating with you or, better, were you and God collaborating in that process? If this was possible in the past, how might it be possible going forward? Spend some time with God considering this possibility Together.

The Invitation:
How Will You Share Your Life with Others in a World of Need?

*"Our life on earth reaches full stature
when it becomes an offering."*

Pope Francis

As he encourages all of humanity to be more concerned about and more generous to others, Pope Francis, history's first Jesuit pope, extends a particular invitation to all of us. He asks us to integrate our own self-realization with the needs of our world and the common good of humanity and our planet. He writes:

> Your own personal vocation does not consist only in the work you do, though that is an expression of it. Your vocation is something more: it is a path guiding your many efforts and actions towards service to others... Contributing to the lives of others gives greater value to everything you do. Your work stops being just about making money, keeping busy or pleasing others. It becomes your vocation because you are called to it; it is something more than merely a pragmatic decision. In the end, it is a recognition of why I was made, why I am here on earth, and what God's plan is for my life. Perhaps I will not be shown every place, time and detail, since I will have to make my own prudent decisions about these. But God will show me a direction in life, and I can let myself be shaped and guided by the One who loves me. Then I will become what I was meant to be, faithful to my own reality. (Pope Francis, *Christ Is Alive*, pars. 255-6)

Reflect on your own talents, passions, and interests. How are they vectored toward contributing to a better world?

Are there ways of deepening your engagement with the voiceless and creating hope for those left behind?

What communal resources do you have that will help you sustain your passion to contribute to a better world?

Committing Yourself
to Ongoing Growth and Renewal

Thinking through the Four Weeks of the Exercises, what did you learn about yourself, about God, about the world, and about your purpose?

What do you still want to learn, understand, and experience in order to keep growing?

What did you learn about how you might change your daily routine in support of these learnings?

With what you now know, do you feel motivated to do something new?

Describe some of the things (people, practices, habits, contexts) that help you to sustain your strength, courage, wisdom, integrity and generosity of spirit.

How can you increase your exposure to those people, practices, and habits in the days to come?

Gillian T.W. Ahlgren

Some Resources for Further Reading

Dean Brackley, *The Call to Discernment in Troubled Times*. New York: Crossroad, 2004.

Katherine Dyckman, Mary Garvin, and Elizabeth Liebert, *The Spiritual Exercises Reclaimed: Uncovering Liberating Possibilities for Women*. Mahwah, NJ: Paulist Press, 2001.

David Fleming, *Draw Me into Your Friendship: A Literal Translation and A Contemporary Reading of the Spiritual Exercises*. St. Louis: Institute of Jesuit Sources, 1996.

Timothy Gallagher, *The Discernment of Spirits: An Ignatian Guide for Everyday Living*. New York: Crossroad, 2005.

Ronald Modras, *Ignatian Humanism: A Dynamic Spirituality for the 21ˢᵗ Century*. Chicago: Loyola Press. 2004.

Antonio T. De Nicolás, *Powers of Imagining: Ignatius de Loyola. A Philosophical Hermeneutic of Imagining through the Works of Ignatius de Loyola with a translation of these works*. Albany: State University of New York. 1986.

John O'Malley, "Ignatius Loyola: Theologian" in Carter Lindberg, ed., *The Reformation Theologians: An Introduction to Theology in the Early Modern Period*, Wiley Blackwell, 2001.

_____, *The Jesuits: A History from Ignatius to the Present*. New York: Rowman and Littlefield, 2017.

About the Author

Gillian T. W. Ahlgren is Professor Emerita of Theology at Xavier University, where she began teaching in 1990. She received her Ph.D. from the University of Chicago in the History of Christianity with a specialization in the Christian mystical tradition, and she has an avid interest in spiritual practices that support personal and social transformation. *Spiritual Exercises for the 21st Century: A Workbook* is her seventh book. Previous books include *Teresa of Avila and the Politics of Sanctity* (Cornell University Press, 1996), *Entering Teresa of Avila's Interior Castle: A Reader's Companion* (Paulist Press, 2005), *The Inquisition of Francisca: A Sixteenth-Century Visionary on Trial* (University of Chicago Press, 2005), *Enkindling Love: The Legacy of Teresa of Avila and John of the Cross* (Fortress Press, 2016) and *The Tenderness of God: Reclaiming Our Humanity* (Fortress Press, 2017).

Dr. Ahlgren has been engaged in pastoral work at a variety of levels. After training in spiritual direction at the Center for Religious Development in 2005, she began to do more targeted workshops and retreat work, especially with those at the margins. In 2009 she was a founding member of the Cincinnati Women's Team of the Ignatian Spirituality Project, a national organization providing spiritual accompaniment for formerly homeless women in recovery from substance abuse. For over ten years she has also worked with women who have survived domestic violence. These and other forms of community engagement have deeply informed her appreciation of Ignatius Loyola's Spiritual Exercises.

Spiritual Exercises for the 21st Century: A Workbook is one of many fruits of a collaborative project on the Exercises begun in 2013. A graduate course by the same name is offered through Xavier University's Institute for Spirituality and Social Justice, which Dr. Ahlgren founded in 2014. Dr. Ahlgren is available to facilitate workshops, training programs, or retreats. Please contact her at ahlgren@xavier.edu.

About Resources for Renewal

Resources for Renewal is an educational 501(c)3 offering programming in renewal, reflection, immersion and discernment. Using tools from the Christian mystical tradition, we promote greater access to human resilience using insights from spiritual leaders and contemplative practices.

We seek to support strong leaders and to nurture the strength of communities, so that the work of discernment, stewardship, and pastoral accompaniment is shouldered together, and so that all can participate in and share the joys of growth and human fruition.

We provide onsite workshops and retreats and offer Spiritual Immersion Experiences in Assisi, Avila, and Montserrat.

About VITALITY

VITALITY is a circle of friends welcoming all, awakening each other, and reminding each other that we are Whole. Our affordable self-care programs invite everyone to move, to breathe, to rest, to contemplate, to grow…wherever each person begins their self-care journey, wherever and however they want to become.

It's the power of a circle!

We invite you to explore with us through our

donation-based classes…in person & via Zoom
affordable trainings
individual sessions
volunteer opportunities

vitalitycincinnati.org

buzz, bliss + books

publishing books from VITALITY's circle of friends
inspiring love, creativity, + possibility

vitalitybuzz.org

www.ingramcontent.com/pod-product-compliance
Lightning Source LLC
Chambersburg PA
CBHW061700120626
46550CB00003B/1026